Date: 6/20/14

J 799.1 FRI
Friesen, Helen Lepp,
Fishing /

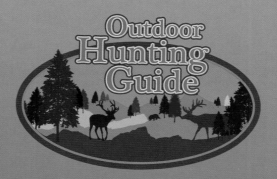

Outdoor
Hunting
Guide

Fishing

Helen Lepp Friesen

MEDIA ENHANCED BOOKS
AV2 BY WEIGL
ADDED VALUE • AUDIO VISUAL

www.av2books.com

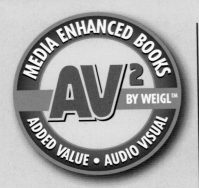

AV² provides enriched content that supplements and complements this book. Weigl's AV² books strive to create inspired learning and engage young minds in a total learning experience.

Your AV² Media Enhanced books come alive with...

 Audio
Listen to sections of the book read aloud.

 Key Words
Study vocabulary, and complete a matching word activity.

 Video
Watch informative video clips.

 Quizzes
Test your knowledge.

Go to **www.av2books.com**, and enter this book's unique code.

BOOK CODE

D 1 8 7 4 2 8

 Embedded Weblinks
Gain additional information for research.

 Slide Show
View images and captions, and prepare a presentation.

AV² by Weigl brings you media enhanced books that support active learning.

 Try This!
Complete activities and hands-on experiments.

... and much, much more!

Published by AV² by Weigl
350 5th Avenue, 59th Floor
New York, NY 10118
Website: www.weigl.com   www.av2books.com

Library of Congress Cataloging-in-Publication Data

Friesen, Helen Lepp, 1961-
Fishing / Helen Lepp Friesen.
    p. cm.
Includes bibliographical references and index.
ISBN 978-1-61913-503-1 (hard cover : alk. paper) — ISBN 978-1-61913-507-9 (soft cover : alk. paper) — ISBN 978-1-61913-698-4 (ebook)
1. Fishing--Juvenile literature. I. Title.
SH445.F75 2013
639.2—dc23
                           2012005578

Printed in the United States of America in North Mankato, Minnesota
3 4 5 6 7 8 9   17 16 15 14 13

112013
WEP05112013

Project Coordinator: Aaron Carr
Art Director: Terry Paulhus

Every reasonable effort has been made to trace ownership and to obtain permission to reprint copyright material. The publishers would be pleased to have any errors or omissions brought to their attention so that they may be corrected in subsequent printings.

Weigl acknowledges Getty Images as its primary image supplier for this title.

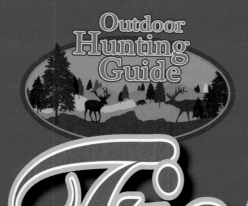

Fishing

Contents

What Is Fishing?

Fishing is catching fish for food and sport. People who fish are sometimes called anglers. Anglers fish in lakes, ponds, oceans, rivers, or seas. People also catch fish in fisheries. A fishery is a place where fish are raised so they can be caught.

Many people fish to get food. Some people catch fish as part of their job. People catch fish in many ways. Anglers fish with a rod, line, and hook. When an angler places mock flies on the hook, it is called fly-fishing. Another way to catch fish is to use a spear. Some people use nets to collect fish, while others catch fish with their bare hands. Many people also fish for fun. Fishing is one of the favorite pastimes of people in North America.

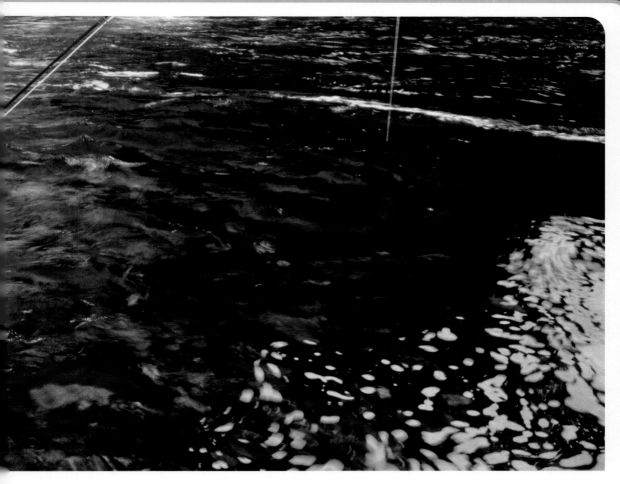

Some people like to fish on weekends or when they are on vacation. It gives them the chance to enjoy nature away from a busy life. Families and friends can relax and spend time together outside. Anglers of all kinds need special gear and fishing licenses. They also need to know how to use the gear.

Fishing For FACTS

There are more than 3,000 kinds of fish that live in North America's water **habitats**.

Freshwater fishing is often said to be the most popular sport in the United States.

The most popular freshwater fish for anglers to catch is the largemouth bass.

Focus on Fishing

In North America, some of the most popular fish that anglers learn to look for are salmon, flounder, and bass. Fishing seasons, the times when people are allowed to catch fish, are determined by local governments. By allowing fishing only at certain times, officials make sure that anglers do not catch too many fish.

Freshwater fish can be found in a lake, an **estuary**, a pond, or a river. They can be caught from a boat, the shore, or a dock. **Saltwater** fishing can be done in shallow coastal waters or in deep seas. Most fish are **cold blooded**, but that does not mean they like the same water temperature. Some are attracted to warm water. Others prefer cold water habitats.

There are many factors an angler thinks about when choosing a place to fish. He or she studies which kind of fish can be found in an area. Successful fishers know where and why some fish move when the seasons change. Anglers study the temperature, currents, and winds.

The best fishing spots are places where fish are looking for food. The shorelines of lakes and rivers have plant life, tiny insects, and small fish. Plants, insects, and small fish are food for bigger fish. Knowing the kind of **bait** each fish prefers is important. The bait must attract the fish away from the other food in the water.

Rainbow trout are related to salmon and native to North America.

Popular Fish

Coho Salmon

Coho salmon eat **plankton** when young and small fish when grown. Coho salmon are found throughout the Pacific Northwest.

Summer Flounder

Summer flounder eat small fish, worms, and other water creatures. Summer flounder are found along the eastern coast of North America.

Largemouth Bass

Largemouth bass eat smaller fish, worms, frogs, insects, and crayfish. Largemouth bass are found across most of North America.

Trout

Trout live in clear, cold lakes and streams. They eat insects such as midges, dragonflies, mayflies, caddis flies, and stoneflies. Trout are found throughout North America.

Pike

Pike live in fresh waters, in weedy or rocky areas close to shore. They eat carp, other small fish, frogs, rats, and small water birds. Pike are found in most parts of North America.

American Indians fished on the Columbia River in the Pacific Northwest.

History

Ancient Chinese, Greek, Egyptian, and Roman writings mention fishing. Long ago, fishing was seen as a means for survival, not as a sport. For many American Indians, fish was a main source of food. Salmon was especially important to the Native People who were living near the shores of the Atlantic and Pacific oceans.

Salmon live in saltwater seas, but they start life in freshwater rivers and lakes. When it is time to **spawn**, the salmon return to the river or lake where they were born. The return is called a salmon run. During the run, fishers know to wait for them. When Native People caught the first salmon during a run, they would perform a ceremony. This was done to express their welcome and thanks. The people then dried and smoked most of the salmon they caught. They stored it for winter food.

Some of the earliest humanmade tools were made for fishing. Before the invention of the fishhook, anglers used a gorge. A gorge was made of wood, bone, or stone sharpened at both sides. It was attached to a line and covered with bait. The fish swallowed the gorge. Then, the angler pulled in the fish. Later, metal fishhooks where invented.

In the 17th century, anglers improved their **tackle** and methods. They learned to tie a loop to the end of the rod. This made it easier to cast the line. In the 1650s, a needle maker named Charles Kirby made changes to the fishhook. The Kirby hook ends in a point that bends outward. It is still used today.

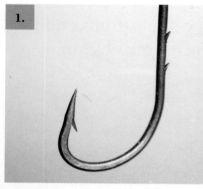

1.

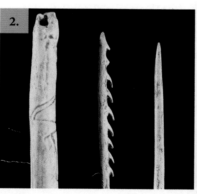

2.

3.

1. Hooks come in different sizes and weights.
2. The tools that early people used for hunting and fishing were often made of bone.
3. Modern tackle is often made of plastic.

TIMELINE

4,000 years ago
Both angling and fishing with nets were shown in drawings made by ancient Egyptians.

1,900 years ago
Claudius Aelianus of Rome wrote about fly-fishing in *On the Nature of Animals*.

600 years ago British royalty started to practice fishing as a sport, as opposed to fishing for food.

360 years ago
Izaak Walton published *The Compleat Angler*, a well-known guide to fishing.

360–350 years ago
Needle maker Charles Kirby invented and improved the Kirby bend fishhook.

330 years ago Early fishing reels, which first came into use in Europe, were plain wooden spools that stored fishing line.

80 years ago
Fiberglass was first produced for commercial use. It was soon used for rods and other gear.

Finding Fish

Successful anglers learn the features of each kind of fish. For example, walleye can see well in faint light. Many other fish cannot. Walleye hunt in dim light, when they can see better than their prey. Largemouth bass enjoy warm temperatures. As a result, largemouth bass are out on a sunny day.

The features include the fish's habitat. The northern pike enjoys cool, shallow water. It is most often found during the spring, after the ice melts. When the weather gets too hot, it leaves.

Many experienced anglers are happy to share what they know. They will tell new fishers to look for weeds, logs, and rocks in water, because many fish will search around those structures for food. When it is hot, look for shady spots. When it is cold, look for spots of sun. There are maps of the best fishing spots. Books and websites explain where fish can be found at each time of year.

The fake flies used in fly-fishing are so light that it takes special skill to cast them across the water.

Fish Features

Fish can be identified by their coloring and other features that make them look different from other kinds of fish. Fish come in many sizes and have different needs. Every **species** of fish prefers certain temperatures, habitats, seasons, and bait. Learning these preferences will help an angler to catch fish.

Blue Marlin

Look for the pointed upper jaw. Bait for this fish can include artificial lures or small tuna.

Salt Water

Catfish

Look for the whiskerlike organs near the mouth. Bait can include dog food.

Fresh Water

Carp

Look for the large mouth, which forms a flattened circle. Bait for carp can include dough and corn.

Fresh Water

Smallmouth Bass

Look for the up-and-down stripes on the sides. Bait for this bass can include artificial grubs or live worms.

Fresh Water

Rainbow Trout

Look for the rainbow scales along the sides of the body. Bait for this trout can include night crawlers.

Fresh Water

Equipment and Clothing

An angler carefully chooses a fishing rod and line. Rough, rocky conditions call for heavier line. Clear water calls for finer, clear line. The angler also packs bobbers and sinkers. A bobber is a small float attached to the fishing line. It helps to keep the hook at a certain depth in the water. When the bobber sinks, the angler knows that a fish has bitten. A sinker is a weight used to sink the bait. Bait alone is too light to sink into the water.

What to Wear

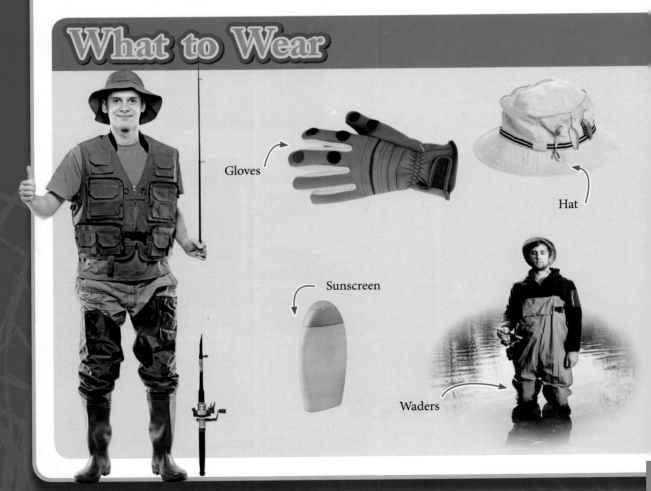

Gloves

Hat

Sunscreen

Waders

Bait may include worms, crickets, grubs, dough balls, or minnows. A lure is bait made to look and move like fish prey. Lures have hooks to catch the fish that bite. Anglers also carry extra line and needle nose pliers, which are used to help remove hooks from fish.

When fishing in warm weather, it is important to wear a hat and loose clothing that covers the skin for sun protection. When fishing in cold weather, it is important to wear warm, waterproof clothing. A flotation suit can keep the angler warm and afloat in case of an accident. Gloves can help anglers keep a better grip on their fishing rods. Some gloves are fingerless to allow the angler to tie knots and bait hooks more easily.

Tools of the Trade

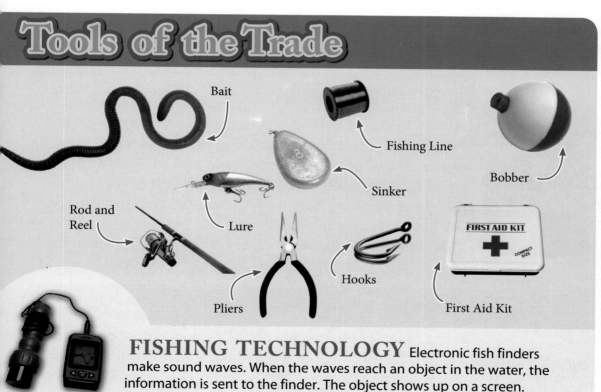

Bait

Fishing Line

Bobber

Sinker

Rod and Reel

Lure

Hooks

First Aid Kit

Pliers

FISHING TECHNOLOGY Electronic fish finders make sound waves. When the waves reach an object in the water, the information is sent to the finder. The object shows up on a screen.

The finder shows the object's size, distance, and location. Some fish finders use the shape to identify the type of fish. Some of the newer fish finders produce clear images of the fish and also include maps.

Safety

Fishing is not usually a dangerous sport. Anglers need to know how to prevent accidents, however. Here are some basic safety tips.

Equipment Safety

It is important to handle fishhooks carefully. This helps prevent injury. When removing a hook from a fish, anglers must be careful to not get the hook caught on their own fingers. Never stand up in a small boat or canoe. Wear footwear that does not slip. Be careful not to load the boat or canoe with more people or gear than the boat can safely carry.

Environmental Safety

Fishing means spending time around water, so one of the biggest dangers is drowning. Always wear a **personal flotation device (PFD)**. People who fish should also know how to swim. Another danger in cold water or weather is a condition called **hypothermia**. When people are too cold for too long, their body temperature can drop. The best way to deal with hypothermia is to prevent it from happening. To fish in the cold, a special covering called a dry suit is recommended.

Weather Safety

If fog covers the water, wait until it clears before going fishing. Take a cell phone or radio to call for help if needed. Always bring along flashlights, which can be used to make signals in case of trouble. Do not go out on water that is too rough. Stay ashore during storms, especially when there might be lightning.

Safety in Numbers

It is safer to fish with other people. Accidents can happen, no matter how careful people are. If one person is injured, another person can help the injured person recover. He or she can also call for help, should it be needed. A fisher should tell others where he or she is going and when to expect a return.

Be Sure of Conditions

People should always be careful when wading into water. It is important to know that clear water is usually deeper than it appears. A current may seem slow when water is only ankle deep. ,When water is waist deep, however, the current can be very strong. If the boat or canoe turns over, hang on to it. Try to move the boat to shallow water.

Fishing For FACTS

- There are almost 40 million anglers in the United States.

- More than 8 million of U.S. anglers are between the ages of 6 and 15.

- Sales of fishing licenses in the United States total nearly $650 million each year. Anglers in Florida tend to spend the most money on fishing.

FISHING CHECKLIST

1. fishing license
2. personal flotation device (PFD)
3. fishing rod and reel
4. hooks
5. fishing line
6. bait
7. lures
8. proper clothing, such as waders
9. extra clothing, in case you get wet
10. fillet knife
11. fishing net
12. cooler with ice for fish
13. insect repellent
14. sunscreen
15. flashlight
16. trash bags
17. whistle
18. flares

Even on public land, officials must approve of the spot where anglers fish.

Fishing Responsibly

There are rules to follow when fishing. Some of the rules are official, such as where fishing is allowed. Anglers must have permission to fish on private land. Other rules are part of being a good sport. For example, anglers should clean up after themselves. The garbage they leave behind can be dangerous. Birds or other animals can get caught in old fishing line. Leaving used fishhooks on a beach can harm people and animals.

Having the right kind of license is important. It is also the angler's responsibility to know the rules of the area. For example, largemouth and smallmouth bass spawn each spring. They have shallow nests, so these fish are easier to find and capture at that time. For that reason, some places do not allow fishing during the spring. There may also be rules about the number of fish an angler is allowed to catch. There may be a top number of fish that can be caught in one season or in one catch.

Some anglers compete in catch and release contests.

Catch and release fishing must be done carefully. In this type of fishing, an angler unhooks the fish that are caught. The fish are released back into the water. Some anglers fish this way as a sport. When catching and releasing, it is important that the fish survive. Anglers need to be careful when catching, weighing, and releasing the fish. It matters where and how the fish is hooked. Fish cannot survive some kinds of injuries. Using bait usually leads to more serious injury. The use of lures or flies is less harmful.

Fishing Careers

Commercial Fisher

A commercial fisher catches fish to be sold to food companies, stores, and restaurants. The work is done on fishing boats, by setting out large nets, sometimes baited with hooks. Fishers work with a crew of people. The crew can be away from home for weeks at a time. A commercial fisher must know how to read maps, compasses, and charts showing water depth. He or she must also know how to operate the boat.

The Rules

Most places have officials who protect the animals in the area. Not all places and officials have the same rules. Anglers must follow the rules of each area where they fish. The angler is responsible for finding out what the rules are. In each area, some seasons are closed to fishing. To see which rules to follow, anglers can look online. They can also read rulebooks to know what is expected of them.

Experienced anglers are a good source of information.

The people who live in an area often have more rights than people from outside. Yet in most cases people need a license to go freshwater fishing. These licenses can usually be bought at a tackle shop. They can also be ordered online. Another kind of license may be needed to catch fish that **migrate**, such as salmon.

Fishing rules can often be found online.

Some fishing methods are against the law. The people who use them can be given a fine. They can even be placed in jail. In some places, it is illegal to shoot at fish with guns. Before going fishing, it is important to be aware of the rules to follow. Quite often, saltwater fishing does not require a license. Yet it is important to check for certain before heading out on the seas. The United States Fish and Wildlife Service has a map that can help. It gives information about fishing in each state. Some species of fish are **endangered**. These kinds of fish are usually off-limits to everyone.

- More than 30 U.S. states have agreed that if a hunting, fishing, or trapping license is taken away from someone by one state, then those privileges are lost in all states for the same amount of time. This is called the Wildlife Violator Compact.
- The American Sportfishing Association works to make sure anglers have plenty of places to fish in clean water.

After Fishing

After catching a fish, an angler can release it back to the water or keep it for food. Some anglers release fish that are too small. Others release fish because they catch them for sport rather than food. When keeping a fish for food, it is important to place the catch in a cooler with ice and salt water so that it does not spoil. Larger fish take longer to chill. Anglers must remove a fish's scales and guts. The sooner a fish is cleaned and cut, the fresher it will taste.

Some anglers enjoy taking pictures of themselves holding their catch. Others may choose to have a record fish stuffed and mounted as a trophy of their great catch, in areas where it is legal to do so.

Sweet Barbecued Salmon

Ingredients
⅓ cup (75 milliliters) lemon juice
¼ teaspoon (1 gram) black pepper
½ teaspoon (2 g) garlic powder
⅓ cup (75 ml) soy sauce
⅓ cup (60 g) brown sugar
⅓ cup (75 ml) water
2 tablespoons (30 ml) vegetable oil
1½ pounds (0.7 kilograms) salmon fillets

Directions
1. In a small bowl, make a marinade. Stir together the lemon juice, pepper, garlic powder, soy sauce, brown sugar, water, and vegetable oil.
2. Place the salmon in a plastic zip bag or container.
3. Add the marinade. Turn the fillets to coat them.
4. Refrigerate the fish for at least 2 hours.
5. Set the barbecue on medium heat. Allow it to preheat for 5 minutes.
6. Oil the barbecue grill lightly. Place the salmon on the grill, and discard the marinade. Cook the salmon for 6 to 8 minutes on each side, until the fish easily flakes with a fork.

Fishing Report

Now, it is your turn to go to work. Choose one of the fish listed in the chart on page 7 of this book, or select another type of fish that anglers often pursue. Using this book, your school or local library, and the internet, write a report about catching this fish.

Research tips:
Look for additional books about fishing in your library under the Dewey Decimal number 799.1.

Useful search terms for the internet include: "fishing and angling" plus the name

of your state or province, "saltwater fishing," "freshwater fishing," or "ice fishing" if appropriate.

Key questions to answer:

1. Where is this fish found?
2. What are the features of this fish?
3. What equipment do you need to catch this fish?
4. What bait attracts this fish?
5. When can you fish for this fish?
6. What licenses are required?

Reel It in Quiz

1 List four things an angler needs to go fishing.

2 Where are the best spots for fishing?

3 How many anglers are there in the United States?

4 What kind of fish comes back to the place it was born?

5 What is a PFD?

6 What is a flotation suit?

7 How many species of fish live in North America's water habitats?

8 In what kind of fishing does the angler place the fish back in the water?

ANSWERS

1. rod, line, bait, and hook 2. where fish find food 3. about 40 million 4. salmon 5. a personal flotation device 6. a waterproof suit that keeps a person warm and afloat after an accident in water 7. about 3,000 8. catch and release

Key Words

bait: something attached to the fishhook to attract fish

cold blooded: having a body temperature that changes in response to the environment

endangered: existing in such small numbers that it is in danger of no longer living in the world

estuary: a water passage where a sea tide sea meets a river current

freshwater: living in water that is not salty

habitats: areas where living things find what they need to grow

hypothermia: the state of an animal's body that has been exposed to cold for a long time

migrate: to move from one place to another in response to weather or other changes

personal flotation device (PFD): a life jacket

plankton: tiny animal and plant life that floats in water

saltwater: living in water that is salty

spawn: to lay fish eggs

species: groups of individuals with common characteristics

tackle: an angler's fishing equipment, such as hooks, extra line, lures, bait, bobbers

Index

Log on to www.av2books.com

AV² by Weigl brings you media enhanced books that support active learning. Go to www.av2books.com, and enter the special code found on page 2 of this book. You will gain access to enriched and enhanced content that supplements and complements this book. Content includes video, audio, weblinks, quizzes, a slide show, and activities.

Audio
Listen to sections of the book read aloud.

Video
Watch informative video clips.

Embedded Weblinks
Gain additional information for research.

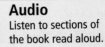

Try This!
Complete activities and hands-on experiments.

WHAT'S ONLINE?

Try This!	**Embedded Weblinks**	**Video**	**EXTRA FEATURES**
Complete a fish-finding activity.	Learn more about fishing.	Watch a video about fishing.	**Audio** Listen to sections of the book read aloud.
Identify game fish.	Find the fishing rules for your state.	Watch a video about fish.	**Key Words** Study vocabulary, and complete a matching word activity.
Try this matching activity for fishing equipment.	Read more about fishing safety.		**Slide Show** View images and captio and prepare a presenta
Test your knowledge of fishing.			**Quizzes** Test your knowledge.

AV² was built to bridge the gap between print and digital. We encourage you to tell us what you like and what you want to see in the future.
Sign up to be an AV² Ambassador at www.av2books.com/ambassador.